# CONTENTS

# What are islands?

Islands are areas of land completely surrounded by water. Although islands are smaller than continents, some islands are huge, covering many thousands of square kilometres. Other islands are just dots in the ocean or areas of land found in lakes and rivers.

## ISLAND VARIETY

Islands are incredibly diverse. Some have soaring mountains, while others are low and rounded. Some are densely forested, while others are grassy or bare. Islands form in several different ways, but the two main types are called continental and oceanic (see pages 6–9). Some islands are found in groups called archipelagos, while others run in long chains.

Islands such as Hong Kong are home to millions of people. The natural landscape has been transformed by urban development, including high-rise buildings.

# GEOGRAPHY NOW

# ISLANDS

## AROUND THE WORLD

## JEN GREEN

First published in 2008 by Wayland

This paperback edition published
by Wayland in 2012

Wayland
Hachette Children's Books
338 Euston Road
London NW1 3BH

Wayland Australia
Level 17/207 Kent Street
Sydney, NSW 2000

Managing Editor: Rasha Elsaeed
Produced by Tall Tree Ltd
Editor: Jon Richards
Designer: Ben Ruocco
Consultant: John Williams

British Library Cataloguing in Publication Data

Green, Jen
  Islands around the world. - (Geography now)
  1. Islands - Juvenile literature 2. Geomorphology -
  Juvenile literature
  I. Title
  551.4'2

ISBN 9780750267953

Printed in China

Wayland is a division of Hachette Children's Books,
an Hachette UK company.

www.hachette.co.uk

## Picture credits

Front cover Dreamstime.com/Wolfgang Amri, 1 istockphoto.com/Martin Maun, 4-5 Dreamstime.com/ Ian Bracegirdle, 4br Dreamstime.com/Mika Makkonen, 5br courtesy of NASA, 6-7 courtesy of NASA, 6bl Dreamstime.com/Sharpshot, 7br courtesy of NASA, 8-9 courtesy of NASA, 9br Dreamstime.com/Albo, 10-11 Dreamstime.com/Greg Pelt, 10bl Dreamstime.com/David Lloyd, 11br Dreamstime.com/Lior Filshteiner, 12-13 Dreamstime.com/Andrew Chambers, 12bl istockphoto.com/Martin Maun,13bc courtesy of NASA, 13br courtesy of US Department of Energy, 14-15 istockphoto.com/Alexander Hafemann, 14bl Dreamstime.com/Gian Marco Valente, 15br Yomangani, 16-17 istockphoto.com/ Rob Broek, 16bl Staffan Widstrand/CORBIS, 17br Erik Torpegaard, 18-19 Dreamstime.com/Gary Hartz, 19cr istockphoto/Kristian Larsen, 19br istockphoto/Ian Campbell, 20-21 istockphoto.com/Jivko Kazakov, 20bl courtesy of NASA, 21br istockphoto.com/Jiri Vatka, 22-23 istockphoto.com/Joshua Haviv, 22b courtesy of the Library of Congress, 23br courtesy of NASA, 24-25 Wayne Lawler; Ecoscene/CORBIS, 24bl istockphoto.com/Omar Ariff, 25br Dreamstime.com/Bernard Breton, 26-27 Dreamstime.com/Dennis Sabo, 26br istockphoto.com/narvikk, 27br ANURUDDHA LOKUHAPUARACHCHI/Reuters/Corbis, 28-29 Dreamstime.com/Sitha Suppalertpisit, 28bl Dreamstime.com/Hans-Thomas Müller, 29br Dreamstime.com/Andy Heyward

*Some islands are uninhabited. In the crowded modern world, such places can often be vital refuges for wildlife. This is one of the Whitsunday Islands off the coast of Australia.*

# ISLAND ENVIRONMENTS

Islands are special places that are often homes to unusual plants and animals. Since ancient times, people have been attracted to islands and have chosen to settle on them – but human settlements have put natural habitats at risk. Today, some of the world's greatest cities, such as New York City and Hong Kong, are located on islands.

## Strategic locations

*Some islands or island groups, such as Japan, form a separate country. Others, such as Hong Kong, are part of another country (China). New Guinea is divided between nations. Some islands have strategic importance. Malta, for example, has been used as a military base for centuries.*

The Mediterranean island of Malta has been claimed by the Arabs, Normans, French and British at various points in history. It is now the smallest nation in the European Union (EU).

# Continental islands

Many of the world's largest islands are continental islands. These islands lie close to mainlands. They rise from the broad, flat ledges that surround the great landmasses, called continental shelves. The waters here are shallow, less than 200 m (660 ft) deep.

## CUT OFF FROM MAINLANDS

Continental islands were once part of mainlands. They were cut off by rising seas or when the land between them sank or subsided. During the last Ice Age, Britain was joined to mainland Europe. During this cold era, sea levels were lower because a lot of water was frozen. As the climate warmed about 18,000 years ago, ice melted, swelling the oceans. The sea rose and Britain became an island.

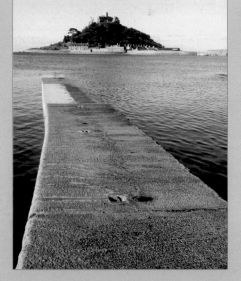

*Tidal islands, such as St Michael's Mount in Cornwall, are part-time islands – entirely surrounded by water only at high tide. At low tide, a causeway links the island to the mainland.*

## MOVING LAND

Some continental islands lie a long way from the nearest continent, separated due to a process called plate tectonics. The Earth's outer crust is made up of a number of huge slabs called tectonic plates. These plates drift very slowly over hot, liquid rock below. Over millions of years, this plate movement carries islands far from the landmasses to which they once belonged.

This map shows the outline of Europe during the last Ice Age (dotted black line) compared with the outline today. Dry land connected Britain with mainland Europe until about 18,000 years ago. Britain became an island when the sea level rose to flood the low-lying land between it and France.

Britain

EUROPE

France

## Barrier islands

*Barrier islands are long, narrow, low-lying islands that usually run parallel to coastlines. They are made of sand, mud or gravel, called sediment, that has been carried out to sea by rivers. Tides and currents dump the sediment in one place, where it piles up to form an island.*

Long, thin barrier islands run for hundreds of kilometres off the east coast of North America, as shown here (left) off the coast of North Carolina.

# Oceanic islands

Oceanic islands are usually small. They have never been connected to a continent, and often lie far out in the open sea. Many oceanic islands are the tops of underwater volcanoes and are made from a volcanic rock called basalt.

*Most volcanic islands rise from the sea near the borders of tectonic plates, but the islands of Hawaii lie at a point called a hot spot, in the middle of a tectonic plate.*

## PILES OF LAVA

Most oceanic islands formed as a result of volcanic activity. They began life when molten rock from deep underground erupted from cracks in the seabed. As time went on, this molten rock (or lava) built up to form a submerged, cone-shaped peak called a seamount. Eventually, the heap of lava broke the ocean surface and became an island.

*Most volcanoes, shown as red dots, lie along plate edges, shown in yellow. A ring of volcanoes runs around the edge of the Pacific Plate. It is called the Ring of Fire.*

## ISLANDS ON PLATE EDGES

Most oceanic islands lie along the edges where two tectonic plates meet. Where plates drift apart in mid-ocean, lava wells up to form an undersea ridge. The highest peaks may break the ocean's surface to form islands. In other places, ocean plates collide, and one slides below the other. The crust melts when it is underground and surges up to the ocean surface to form a line of islands.

North America

Asia

Europe

Africa

PACIFIC PLATE

South America

Australasia

# Coral islands

*Coral reefs and islands are made of billions of skeletons! These are the chalky skeletons of very small sea creatures called coral polyps. These tiny animals thrive in the warm, shallow waters off tropical islands. If a volcanic island later sinks or collapses, it leaves behind a hollow ring of coral called a coral atoll.*

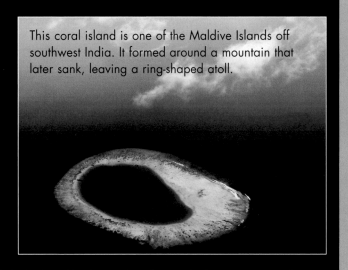

This coral island is one of the Maldive Islands off southwest India. It formed around a mountain that later sank, leaving a ring-shaped atoll.

# Climate and wildlife

Many islands have a mild, wet climate. This is because ocean breezes cool the island in summer and warm it in winter, while moist ocean winds bring rain. Many islands have unique plants and animals that are not found on the nearest mainland.

## ISLAND HABITATS

Islands have different habitats, depending on whether they lie in tropical, temperate or polar waters. The island's rock also affects the landscape, soil and plants. Large islands may have a range of habitats. Madagascar, for example, is a big island off Africa with rainforests, grasslands, dry scrublands, swamps and coral reefs.

*Remote islands are colonised by plant seeds carried by wind or water. This palm-tree seedling (left) is sprouting from a nut that washed up on a tropical lava beach.*

## UNUSUAL WILDLIFE

Remote islands often have an unusual mix of wildlife. Most animals found on oceanic islands arrived by either flying, floating or swimming. For this reason, birds, bats and insects are common, along with water-dwellers such as seals and turtles. Land animals are much rarer. Once they have reached an island, plants and animals evolve (change slowly) to become new species that are better adapted to the conditions in their new environment.

## Unique animals

*Oceanic islands are often home to animals found nowhere else. For example, Madagascar is home to unique mammals called lemurs. These mammals resemble monkeys, but belong to another group of primates. The island also has hedgehog-like creatures called tenrecs, and a unique cat called the fossa.*

Ring-tailed lemurs are one of 30 species of lemur found only on Madagascar.

# How are islands used?

Many islands have rich natural resources such as fish, timber and minerals. Land that can be farmed and settled is often the most precious resource of all. Since ancient times, islands have been settled by humans to make use of these resources.

*Many islands in the tropics have large plantations. Crops such as bananas (below), tea, coffee, rubber and sugar are grown for sale abroad.*

# SETTLEMENTS AND COLONIES

In prehistoric times, remote islands were colonised by seafaring peoples such as the Polynesians of the South Pacific. These original settlers survived by fishing and farming. From the 1500s, European explorers reached and colonised many islands, claiming them for their own countries. Timber, minerals and other resources were harvested and shipped back to Europe.

*The islands of Japan have many large, modern cities such as the port of Kobe, shown here.*

## NEW CHANGES

From the 1800s, industrialisation brought huge changes to some islands. Small settlements grew into modern cities or busy ports with docks and factories. During the last half of the 1900s, tourism became a major industry on many islands. Jet airliners allowed people to fly to remote islands, and hotels spread along the shore.

## Test sites

In the mid-1900s, some oceanic islands were used to test nuclear weapons. The remoteness of the islands made them seem a good choice for weapons tests. In the 1950s, the United States carried out bomb tests on the remote Pacific island of Bikini. Local people were forced to leave the island.

During the 1950s and 1960s, the United States exploded 70 nuclear bombs on Bikini and on another island, Enewetak.

13

# Protecting islands

Islands are fragile environments where the balance of nature is easily upset. Activities such as fishing, farming and mining can threaten local wildlife and damage precious habitats. Conservation is now a top priority on many islands.

## WILDLIFE AT RISK

Hunting and fishing are often important industries on islands, but they also threaten animals such as seals, fish and turtles. In some cases, they have caused extinctions, where species of animals disappear completely. On the Indian Ocean island of Mauritius, a flightless bird called the dodo was hunted to extinction in the 1500s. Tourism can also disturb island wildlife.

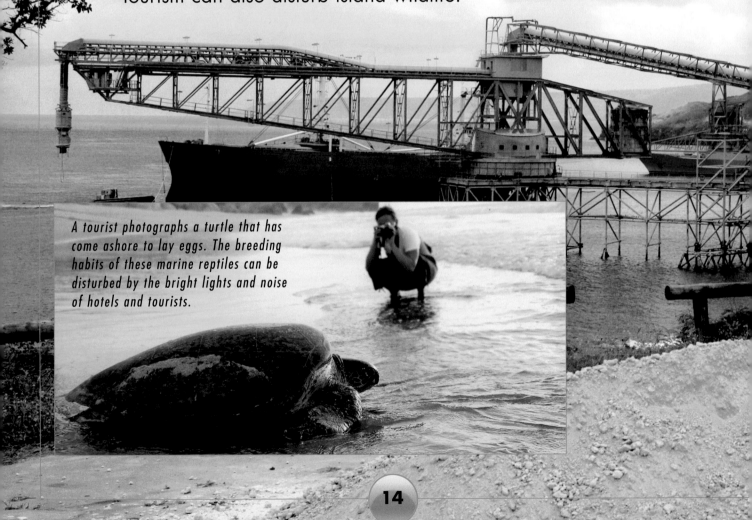

A tourist photographs a turtle that has come ashore to lay eggs. The breeding habits of these marine reptiles can be disturbed by the bright lights and noise of hotels and tourists.

# THREATENED HABITATS

Island habitats are often harmed by farming, forestry and mining. On many islands, forests have been stripped for timber. Native vegetation has been cleared to make way for farms, settlements and sometimes mines. Fortunately, conservation is now a key issue on many islands. Wild habitats have been saved by the establishment of reserves and nature parks.

*Phosphate mining is the main industry on Christmas Island in the Indian Ocean. Like farming and forestry, mining can lead to erosion and cause pollution.*

## Introducing wildlife

*Island wildlife is also threatened when people introduce (bring in) new plants and animals. In the past, sailors often left goats and sheep on islands to provide food. These new animals stripped the local vegetation, leaving little for native plant-eaters. New predators, such as dogs, cats and rats, also prey on island wildlife.*

On the Caribbean island of Cuba, a unique mammal called the hutia has been hunted by introduced predators, such as rats and mongooses. Hutias are now very rare.

# Arctic wilderness

## Greenland

Greenland

**STATISTICS**

- Island type: Continental
- Size: 2,175,000 sq km (840,000 sq miles)
- Population: 56,344 (2007 estimate)
- Capital: Godthab (also known as Nuuk)
- National status: Self-governing province of Denmark
- Main industries: Fishing (also hunting and farming)

Greenland is the world's largest island, covering 2,175,000 square km (840,000 square miles). This continental island was once part of North America. Greenland's cold polar climate and scarce resources mean that relatively few people live there. Most of the island is an untouched wilderness, with a huge nature reserve in the northeast.

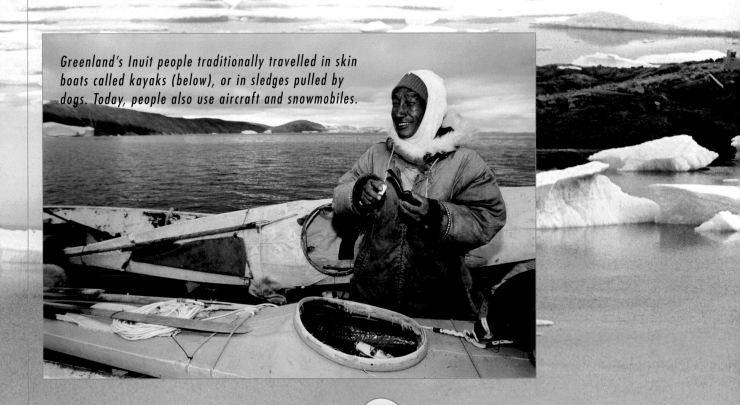

Greenland's Inuit people traditionally travelled in skin boats called kayaks (below), or in sledges pulled by dogs. Today, people also use aircraft and snowmobiles.

## POPULATION

On Greenland there are less than three people for every 100 square kilometres (38 square miles)! The original inhabitants were the Inuit, who arrived from North America about 5,000 years ago. Greenland became a colony of Denmark in the 1300s, but since 1979, the island has been self-governing. The Inuit traditionally live by fishing and hunting. Fishing is the main industry.

## ICY CLIMATE

Much of Greenland lies inside the Arctic Circle. Temperatures range from 10°C (50°F) in summer to -40°C (-40°F) in winter. In summer the Sun never sets, so it is light at midnight. In winter, the Sun never rises. Most of Greenland is covered by an ice cap up to 3 km (2 miles) deep.

*The coasts of Greenland are warmed by the ocean, so their climate is milder than inland. Almost all of the island's inhabitants live in settlements on southern coasts, where a little sheep farming is possible. Pictured below is the town of Kulusuk.*

## Viking colony

*The Vikings were the first Europeans to settle on Greenland. In 985 AD, a Viking leader named Erik the Red landed on the island. Finding green pastures on the coast, Erik named the island Greenland. The Vikings survived on Greenland until the 1400s, when the climate grew colder and they abandoned their villages.*

Viking sailors used this device, called a bearing dial, to navigate across the open ocean to Greenland.

# Island evolution

## Galápagos Islands

Galápagos
Islands

**STATISTICS**

- Island type: Volcanic and oceanic
- Size: 7,844 sq km (3,029 sq miles)
- Population: 20,000 on four islands
- Largest town: Puerto Ayora, Isabela
- National status: Colony of Ecuador
- Main industries: Tourism

The Galápagos are a group of volcanic islands off Ecuador in South America, famous for their unique wildlife. In the 1830s, the British naturalist Charles Darwin visited the islands. The species he saw helped him to develop his ideas on evolution.

## CLIMATE AND WILDLIFE

The Galápagos consist of 15 large islands and many small islets. The climate is quite dry. The islands lie on the Equator, but are cooled by a cold ocean current. Unique wildlife includes a tropical penguin and the marine iguana – the world's only sea-going lizard. There are also giant tortoises.

## HUMAN IMPACT

The Galápagos were discovered in the 1500s. Over the centuries, sailors landed on the islands to hunt for fresh meat, and this reduced seal and tortoise populations. Sailors also left goats, sheep and pigs, which ate the vegetation. The Galápagos became a reserve in 1959 and park fees now help to pay for conservation work.

*Galápagos tortoises are among the world's largest tortoises. They grow to 1.2 m (4 ft) long and can weigh over 200 kg (440 lbs).*

*Thirteen species of finch are found on the Galápagos. Some have stout beaks suitable for cracking seeds, while others have slender bills for catching insects.*

## Charles Darwin

*Charles Darwin studied the wildlife of the Galápagos in 1835. He studied the 13 species of finch that live on the islands, and guessed that all 13 were descended from a single species. This species had spread to the other islands in the Galápagos and evolved beaks of different shapes to eat local foods.*

Darwin's studies of Galápagos finches led him to develop his theory of evolution. He published his ideas in 1859.

# Volcanic dangers

## Santorini

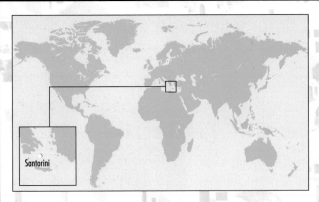

**STATISTICS**

- Island type: Volcanic
- Size: 73 sq km (29 sq miles)
- Population: 11,000 (2002 estimate)
- Largest town: Phira
- National status: Part of Greece
- Main industries: Tourism, wine-growing

Volcanic islands are always at risk from fresh eruptions. People, plants and animals can die if a volcano erupts, spouting red-hot lava and clouds of ash. About 3,500 years ago, an eruption on the Greek island of Santorini brought disaster to the ancient world.

### ERUPTION

Around 2000 BC, Santorini was an outpost of the Minoan Empire, based on the island of Crete to the south. In about 1600 BC, Santorini's volcano exploded, showering ash far and wide. The explosion formed a huge hollow called a caldera, into which seawater gushed. This sent giant waves, called tsunamis, across the ocean. Ash engulfed the town of Akrotiri on Santorini, while cities on Crete were wrecked by giant waves.

*This satellite view shows the main island of Santorini and smaller islands curving around a central bay. This deep bay is the caldera left by the explosion of 1600 BC.*

## THE ISLAND TODAY

After 1500 BC, Santorini became a colony of ancient Greece, Rome and then the Ottoman Empire. In 1912, it became part of the modern state of Greece. The island now has about 11,000 inhabitants. Vines grow well in the volcanic soil, but water is scarce. The main industry on the island is tourism. Holidaymakers visit the ruins of Akrotiri, which have been excavated, or relax on beaches made of black volcanic sand.

## Minoan civilisation

*The Minoans flourished on Crete from 3000 to 1100 BC. The Minoan capital, Knossos, was the centre of a mighty empire. The tsunamis of 1600 BC wrecked coastal cities and broke the power of the Minoans. The disaster may also have inspired the legend of Atlantis, which tells of a beautiful island city under the sea.*

The palace at Knossos has been partly restored. Beautiful wall paintings there show scenes from Minoan life.

# Crowded city

## Manhattan Island

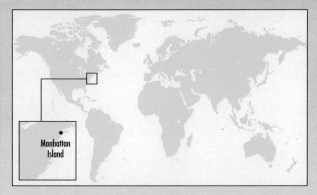

Manhattan Island

**STATISTICS**

- Island type: *Continental*
- Size: *58 sq km (23 sq miles)*
- Population: *1,537,195 (2007 census)*
- National status: *Part of the United States*
- Main industries: *Finance, trade, manufacturing, service industries, tourism*

Around the world, many islands are now intensively settled and developed – and none more so than Manhattan Island, which lies at the heart of New York City. Good transport links are vital on crowded islands. Bridges, tunnels and ferries connect Manhattan with other islands and the mainland.

*This photo shows Manhattan's docks around 1900. Later, the deepwater docks were moved to the mainland. New York is still among the world's 20 largest ports.*

## THE CITY RISES

Manhattan Island lies on a natural harbour at the mouths of the Hudson and East Rivers. In the 1620s, Dutch traders founded the first settlement on this small island. In the 1800s, large docks were built and factories sprang up to process raw materials brought by boat. By 1900, one of the world's largest cities had spread to the surrounding mainland.

## MODERN MANHATTAN

Over 1.5 million people now live on Manhattan Island. On working days, the city's population doubles as people commute in to work. Manhattan Island lies at the heart of America's business capital. It is also a major tourist destination. Visitors come to see Manhattan's parks, museums and shops, as well as landmarks like the Statue of Liberty.

*On crowded islands, the only way to build is up! Manhattan bristles with tall skyscrapers. The Chrysler Building with its graceful spire is currently the city's second-tallest building after the Empire State Building.*

## Central Park

*Manhattan's Central Park provides a much-needed green space in the heart of a bustling, polluted city. Covering 3.4 sq km (1.3 sq miles), the park was laid out in the 1850s. There are playgrounds, sports facilities and two ice rinks. The park is especially peaceful when closed to traffic during the evening and at weekends.*

A satellite view of Central Park's lakes with the buildings of central New York City on either side.

# Rich resources

## New Guinea

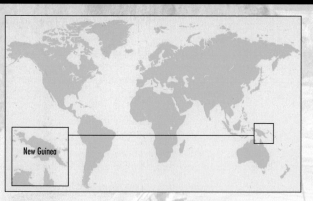

New Guinea

**STATISTICS**

- Island type: Continental
- Size: 818,000 sq km (320,000 sq miles)
- Population: 6.4 million (2000 estimate)
- Largest towns: Port Moresby (PNG), Jayapura (WNG)
- National status: Western New Guinea is part of Indonesia; Papua New Guinea is independent
- Main industries: Farming, forestry, mining

New Guinea in the western Pacific is the world's second-largest island. This landmass is divided between two nations. The western half, Western New Guinea, belongs to Indonesia. The eastern half, Papua New Guinea, is an independent country. The island's rich resources are as yet under-used, but this is changing fast.

### LANDSCAPE AND FIRST SETTLERS

New Guinea is a very mountainous island. Lying just south of the Equator, the low-lying coasts are hot and humid, but the mountains are cooler. Much of the island is covered with dense rainforests, which are home to birds of paradise. Tens of thousands of years ago, New Guinea was settled by Polynesians who arrived in canoes.

*New Guinea wildlife includes birds of paradise (left), tree kangaroos, large birds called cassowaries, and the world's largest butterfly, the Queen Alexandra birdwing.*

*Mining and other industries mean that New Guinea's forests are disappearing rapidly. Heavy rain washes away soil that is no longer held in place by tree roots. This is called erosion.*

## EXPLOITING RESOURCES

New Guinea's natural resources inclu
valuable hardwood. In some areas, h
forest have been felled. Western Nev
large copper mines. Nickel, oil and n
also mined, causing pollution. Papua
was a colony of Britain, then Australi
becoming independent in 1975. In 2
New Guinea gained partial indepen
Indonesia, but many people want ful

## Village life

*Until recently, about half of New Guinea's six million people lived in rural settlements. Villages in the mountains have round, thatched huts. In the lowlands, many houses are built on stilts so they stand above any flooding. More and more people are now moving from inland villages to find work in coastal towns.*

Until recently, the remote hill pe
had little contact with the outsid
hunting, growing sweet potato

Mal

STATISTICS

CORA
The o
came
(435
variou
to Ho
before
1965
indust
Touris
stunni

# reatened paradise

## ldives

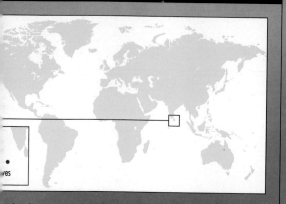

Island type: Coral atolls
Size: 298 sq km (115 sq miles)
Population: 369,031 (2006 estimate) on 200 islands
Capital: Male
National status: Independent republic
Main industries: Tourism, fishing, farming

## L ISLANDS

iginal settlers of the Maldives
from Sri Lanka, 700 km
niles) to the northeast. At
s times the islands belonged
and, Portugal and Britain,
gaining independence in
Fishing used to be the main
y but now it is tourism.
s are attracted by the
g beaches and coral reefs.

The Maldives are a group of coral islands in the Indian Ocean. About 1,200 small islands are grouped into a dozen atolls. White-sand beaches and blue lagoons make this an idyllic holiday destination. However, these low-lying islands are threatened by rising sea levels.

*Male, capital of the Maldives, has been heavily developed. Buildings include several mosques, where the islands' Muslim population worship.*

A diver studies a beautiful but poisonous lionfish – just one of the many colourful species that can be seen on the Maldives' coral reefs.

## RISING SEAS

The Maldives are extremely low-lying, wi height of just 2.3 m (8 ft) above sea leve believe sea levels are now rising worldw Earth is getting warmer, as pollution fron and power stations traps the Sun's heat. caps are melting, which is swelling the c raising sea levels.

C

Ne

New Z

STATISTICS

HUM
New
arrive

## At risk from the waves

In the 1900s, sea levels rose by 20 cm (8 in). If this process continues, much of the Maldives could be underwater by 2100. Another risk comes from large waves, or tsunamis. In 2004, tsunamis caused by an earthquake off southeast Asia washed right over some of the Maldives, causing extensive damage.

The Maldives were badly dama tsunamis, even though the sour thousands of kilometres away.

# nange and conservation

## Zealand

land type: Continental, partly volcanic

ize: 270,534 sq km (104,454 sq miles)

opulation: 4,115,771 (2007 estimate)

apital: Wellington (largest city: Auckland)

ational status: Independent nation

lain industries: Farming, manufacturing, service industries

New Zealand in the southwest Pacific is known for its distinctive wildlife, including several species of flightless birds. In the last 200 years, however, these islands have been changed greatly by human settlement. Native wildlife is threatened, but conservation work is helping to repair the damage done.

## N IMPACT

ealand's first settlers were a Polynesian people called the Maori, who about 1,000 years ago. Europeans began to settle from the 1800s.

New animals introduced by humans included dogs, cats, possums and weasels, which preyed on defenceless island birds. The Europeans also brought sheep and cattle, and cleared forests to make pastures. All these changes threatened native wildlife, and some species became extinct.

*Maori culture is thriving in New Zealand, unlike traditional ways on other islands. Maori meeting houses (left) are used for ceremonies and gatherings.*

# HABITATS AND WILDLIFE

New Zealand consists of two large islands and many smaller ones. The South Island is mainly mountainous with a cool climate, while the North Island is somewhat lower with milder conditions. Isolated from other landmasses for over 150 million years, New Zealand has many unique species, including flightless birds such as the kiwi. Scientists believe these island birds lost the ability to fly because they had very few predators.

*Sheep farming is a major industry in New Zealand. However, these non-native animals have caused widespread erosion as they strip the ground of plants that hold the soil in place.*

## Conserving rare animals

*Conservationists are now working to preserve New Zealand's unique wildlife. Flightless birds and a rare reptile called the tuatara are protected on offshore island sanctuaries. Non-native hunters, such as rats and weasels, have been carefully removed so there is nothing to hunt these endangered animals.*

Tuataras are very unusual reptiles that resemble lizards. They grow to 20 cm (8 in) long and can live for 100 years.

# Glossary and resources

**ARCHIPELAGO**
A large group of islands scattered over a wide expanse of ocean.

**ATOLL**
An island made of coral, often in the form of a ring surrounding a lagoon.

**BARRIER ISLAND**
An island made of sediment dropped by water currents.

**CALDERA**
A hollow that forms when a volcano's cone collapses.

**CAUSEWAY**
A thin strip of land linking an island to the mainland. It may flood at high tide.

**COLONISE**
When people, plants or animals reach and settle on a place such as an island.

**CONSERVATION**
Work done in order to protect nature.

**CONTINENTAL SHELF**
A broad ledge that surrounds a continent, forming a shelf of shallow water.

**EROSION**
The wearing away of the land by wind, water or ice.

**EVOLVE**
When species of living things change slowly to suit their environment.

**EXPLOIT**
To make full use of a resource, sometimes at the risk of damage to the environment.

**EXTINCTION**
When a whole species dies out.

**HABITAT**
A particular place where plants and animals live, such as a forest or a desert.

**HOT SPOT**
A weak point near the centre of a tectonic plate where molten rock bursts through to form volcanoes.

**ICE AGE**
A period in the Earth's history when ice covered more land than it does today.

**ISLET**
A tiny island.

**LAGOON**
A shallow coastal lake.

**LAVA**
Hot, molten rock that erupts from a volcano.

**NATIVE**
Of the original plants, animals or people found on an island.

**POLAR**
To do with the North and South Poles.

**PRIMATE**
A member of the group of mammals that includes apes, monkeys and humans.

**RING OF FIRE**
A ring of volcanoes that runs around the edge of the Pacific Ocean.

**SEAMOUNT**
An undersea mountain, formed by volcanic activity.

**SEDIMENT**
Loose particles of rocky material, such as sand or mud.

**TECTONIC PLATE**
One of the huge, rigid plates that make up the outer layer of the Earth.

**TEMPERATE**
To do with the regions between the tropics and the poles.

**TROPICAL**
To do with the regions that lie on either side of the Equator.

## FURTHER READING
*Earth Files: Islands*, Chris Oxlade
(Heinemann, 2003)
*Ocean Watch*, Martyn Bramwell
(Dorling Kindersley, 2001)
*The World's Top Ten Islands*, Neil Morris
(Anova Books, 2003)

## WEBSITES
www.windows.ucar.edu/tour/link=/earth/interior/plate_tectonics.html
A website describing island formation and plate tectonics.
www.coralreefalliance.org
A website that focuses on coral reefs and islands.
www.nature.org/wherewework/islands
A website that looks at the human use of islands.
www.wwct.org/island_habitats.php
A website that examines the wide variety of island habitats.

# Islands topic web

Use this topic web to discover themes and ideas in subjects that are related to islands.

**GEOGRAPHY**
- The formation of oceanic, continental and barrier islands.
- How coral reefs form.
- How plate tectonics and volcanic activity can shape islands.
- The natural resources found on islands.

**SCIENCE AND THE ENVIRONMENT**
- How plants and animals colonise islands.
- Evolution of island wildlife.
- Impact of people on island environments and conservation work.

**MATHS AND ECONOMICS**
- Calculating the density of island populations, using statistics on island size and population.
- Exploitation of island resources both in the past and today.

**ISLANDS**

**ENGLISH AND LITERACY**
- Stories, myths and legends about islands.
- First-hand accounts of modern life on islands by people who live there.
- Debate the pros and cons of tourist development on remote tropical islands.

**HISTORY**
- The history of exploration and the discovery of various islands.
- Colonisation of islands and the gaining of independence.
- Strategic importance of islands for trade and military use.

# Index